pumpkin

pumpkin

Joanna Farrow

hamlyn

First published in Great Britain in 2003 by Hamlyn,
a division of Octopus Publishing Group Ltd
2-4 Heron Quays, London E14 4JP

ISBN 0 600 60932 4

A CIP catalogue record for this book is available from
the British Library

Printed and bound in China

10 9 8 7 6 5 4 3 2

Acknowledgements:
Executive Editor: Sarah Ford
Editor: Alice Tyler
Executive Art Editor: Joanna MacGregor
Home Economy: Joanna Farrow
Special Photography: Stephen Conroy
Other Photography:
Corbis UK Ltd 7
Octopus Publishing Group Limited/Jeremy Hopley
52/Peter Myers 65/William Reavell 41, 72/Ian Wallace 21

Notes

Standard level spoon measurements are used in all recipes.

Eggs should be large unless otherwise stated. The FDA
advises that eggs should not be consumed raw. This book
contains dishes made with raw or lightly cooked eggs. It is
prudent for vulnerable people such as pregnant and nursing
mothers, invalids, the elderly, babies, and young children to
avoid dishes made with uncooked or lightly cooked eggs.
Once prepared these dishes should be kept refrigerated and
used promptly.

This book includes dishes made with nuts and nut derivatives.
It is advisable for people with known allergic reactions to nuts
and nut derivatives and those who may be potentially
vulnerable to these allergies, such as pregnant and nursing
mothers, invalids, the elderly, babies and children to avoid
dishes made with nuts and nut oils. It is also prudent to check
the labels of pre-prepared ingredients for the possible
inclusion of nut derivatives.

Milk should be whole unless otherwise stated.

Fresh herbs should be used unless otherwise stated. If
unavailable use dried herbs as an alternative, but halve the
quantities stated.

Ovens should be preheated to the specified temperature—if
using a convection oven, follow manufacturer's instructions for
adjusting the time and temperature.

contents

introduction

The bright orange pumpkin, that distinctive symbol of fall, belongs to the family of cucurbits (Cucurbitaceae), trailing vine plants that include squashes, gourds, cucumbers, gherkins, muskmelons, and watermelons. Strictly speaking, pumpkins are fruits rather than vegetables. The flesh has a mild, sweet flavor and is used for both sweet and savory dishes. The seeds can be roasted (see page 9) to make a crunchy, nutritious snack or a garnish for soups and salads. Pumpkin flowers are also edible.

Grown throughout much of the United States, pumpkins take 90–120 days to mature before ripening between late summer and late fall, hence their popularity at this time of the year. As well as being used in cooking—in pies, cookies, bread, stews, and soups to name a few—pumpkins are often used to decorate homes in the fall and winter, especially for Halloween and Thanksgiving. Miniature pumpkins are commonly used as ornaments and can often be seen in autumnal floral displays, while larger ones are hollowed out and carved to make cheery—or spooky—jack o'lanterns. The earliest use for pumpkins was as animal feed and they are still used as such today.

A history of pumpkins

Pumpkins are thought to have originated in Central America thousands of years ago. Spanish and Portuguese adventurers first introduced the seeds to Europe in the 14th century and, as a result, pumpkins are now grown worldwide.

Native Americans in North America had been growing and using pumpkins long before the arrival of colonial settlers in the early 17th century. Besides roasting and eating the pumpkin flesh and the seeds, they used flattened, dried strips of pumpkin shell for making mats, and whole dried pumpkin shells were used as bowls and containers.

Pumpkins also became important for the Pilgrims. This explains the role of pumpkin—usually in the form of pumpkin pie—in today's Thanksgiving celebrations, which annually commemorate the thanks offered to God by the Pilgrims in 1621 following their first successful harvest. The first pumpkin pies were in fact pumpkin shells filled with milk, pumpkin flesh, spices, and maple syrup and baked for hours in hot ashes.

The word "pumpkin" is thought to derive from the classical Greek word *pepon*. Pronounced by the French as *pompon*, this was later anglicized to *pumpion*, and in turn altered by the American colonists to "pumpkin."

Pumpkin varieties

Pumpkins come in myriad shapes, sizes, and varieties, the names of which are probably better known to gardeners than to cooks. Some varieties are better for carving, while others are better for cooking. The best-known varieties are bright orange, ribbed, and round (90 percent of these are sold for Halloween jack o'lanterns), but pumpkins also come in shades of white, yellow, peach, tan, and green, and also stripey combinations of these colors. Sizes range from mini pumpkins the size of a tennis ball that weigh less than 1 pound to jumbo fruits grown for competitions that can weigh over 1000 pounds. The cultivation of these outsized pumpkins is a popular pastime and the gigantic monsters (usually of the Atlantic Giant variety) are judged at pumpkin weigh-offs around the country at harvest time. The current record stands at 1337.6 pounds.

Selecting and storing pumpkins

If you are buying a pumpkin for cooking rather than for decorative purposes, its shape is unimportant. However, it should feel heavy for its size and be free of blemishes and soft spots, which can cause it to spoil prematurely. Although big pumpkins are impressive to look at, the flesh from smaller-sized fruits (the so-called pie, sugar, or sweet pumpkins) is usually sweeter and less watery than that from very large ones. The green-stripey cushaw is a long-necked pumpkin with green stripes, whose unique texture makes it ideal for custards and pies.

If possible, choose a pumpkin with 1–2 inches of stem left, because pumpkins without stems decay more quickly. Miniature pumpkins like the Baby Boo and Jack-Be-Little should be used soon after harvesting or purchasing, but larger, whole pumpkins can be stored at room temperature for up to a month or in a cool dry place for 2–3 months. Once a pumpkin is cut open it is highly perishable. It needs to be tightly wrapped, refrigerated, and used within five days.

Nutritional benefits

Pumpkins are 90 percent water and, like most fruits and vegetables, of great nutritional value. They are low in calories and rich in fiber, vitamins C and E, and potassium. The orange color of pumpkin flesh is a clue to its high content of the carotenoid pigments

lutein, alpha-carotene, and beta-carotene (which turns into vitamin A in the body). Vitamins A, C, and E are powerful antioxidants that help protect the body against free radicals—the highly unstable molecules that cause both minor infections and serious degenerative diseases like cancer and heart disease—as well as conditions that come with premature aging. Pumpkin seeds are a good source of essential fatty acids, protein, iron, and zinc, and are thought to help prevent kidney stones.

Halloween jack o'lanterns

The practice of using pumpkins as lanterns at Halloween derives from an ancient Celtic tradition brought to America by Irish immigrants. All Hallows' Eve on October 31st marked the end of the Celtic year, and it was on this night that the Irish would place hollowed-out turnips, rutabagas, and beets with a light inside in porches and windows. These would welcome the spirits of ancestors into their homes and ward off evil spirits and a restless soul called Stingy Jack.

The story goes that Stingy Jack was a miserable, mean drunk who played tricks on the Devil. When Jack died he was refused entrance to Heaven. The Devil also refused him entry into Hell, sending him away with only a burning lump of coal to light his way. Jack was therefore left to roam the dark world between the two and carried his burning coal inside a hollowed-out turnip.

When the tradition came to America, the larger and more easily carved native pumpkin became the favorite choice for hollowing out and a candle replaced the burning coal.

"Jack o'lantern pumpkin" is now a generic term for the deep orange varieties like the Connecticut Field, the traditional American pumpkin, which is used for making these lanterns. Such varieties have large cavities and thin walls, which make them ideal for carving. Look for a pumpkin with a flat bottom, a hard outer layer with no soft spots, and an intact stem that you can use as a handle for the lid.

To hollow out a pumpkin, first cut out a "lid" that can be replaced. Scrape out the seeds and strings and scoop out the flesh using an ice-cream scoop, which is stronger than an ordinary spoon. Scrape the inside wall of the area to be carved to a thickness of

1 inch. To carve your pumpkin, make sure you stand it on a flat surface and use a sharp knife, always cutting away from your body and using a gentle but firm sawing action. You can carve your pumpkin freehand if you prefer but there are plenty of carving kits containing stencils and saws to help you cut out your chosen design. A light coating of petroleum jelly applied to the cuts will help the pumpkin last longer. Alternatively, you can buy commercial pumpkin protector spray.

Pumpkin puree

Since fresh pumpkins are available only in the fall and early winter, canned and frozen pureed pumpkin are the next best thing and are available all year round. Solid-pack canned puree with no added salt or sugar is just as tasty and nutritious as fresh pumpkin. However, it is easy to make your own puree, which can be kept in the freezer for up to six months ready for use in tarts, pies, and any other recipe that requires solid-pack canned pumpkin. You will need about 1 pound of raw, untrimmed pumpkin to make 1 cup of pumpkin puree.

First remove the stalk then cut the pumpkin in half, using a sharp knife, and scoop out the seeds and strings. The pumpkin can now be boiled, steamed, or baked before pureeing. To boil or steam the pumpkin, cut it into large chunks (peel away the skin now if desired) and place in a saucepan with about 1 cup of water. Cover and boil for 10–15 minutes or until tender, then drain. Alternatively steam the pieces for 15–20 minutes. To bake the pumpkin, simply place the two halves, cut side down, on cookie sheets and bake in a preheated oven at 350°F for 1 hour.

When it is cool enough to handle, remove the pumpkin skin using a sharp knife. Work the flesh to a puree in a food processor or blender, press through a sieve, or use a ricer or potato masher.

Cooking partners

Pumpkin may be prepared in almost any way that is suitable for winter squashes like butternut squash and hubbard squash. Since the flesh absorbs the flavor of whatever it is cooked with, pumpkin goes particularly well with strong flavors—cheese, coriander, spices like chile, ginger, curry powder, and turmeric, and strong meats like chorizo, pancetta, or bacon. For sweet dishes, brown sugar and maple syrup bring out the sweetness of pumpkin, and work well with ground cinnamon or nutmeg.

roasted pumpkin seeds

Instead of throwing away the cupful or so of seeds found in the average-sized pumpkin, try roasting them.

Pull away the fibrous strings around the seeds and wash the seeds well. Pat dry with paper towels.

Toss the dry seeds in a bowl with salt and a little olive oil, vegetable oil, or melted butter. Spread them out in a single layer on a cookie sheet. Bake at 325°F for 15–20 minutes, shaking the cookie sheet occasionally. Leave to cool completely then serve.

appetizers, snacks, and side dishes

pumpkin and apple soup

preparation time: 15 minutes
cooking time: 30 minutes

- ¼ stick (2 tablespoons) butter
- 1 large onion, roughly chopped
- 2 teaspoons chopped fresh thyme
- 2 small cooking apples, peeled, cored, and roughly chopped
- 3 tablespoons dark brown sugar
- 2 tablespoons whole-grain mustard
- 1 small pumpkin, about 1½ lbs, skinned, seeded, and cut into chunks
- 4½ cups vegetable stock
- ½ cup crème fraîche
- salt and pepper
- pumpkin seeds, for sprinkling

1 Melt the butter in a large, heavy-based saucepan. Add the onion and thyme and cook gently, stirring frequently, until softened and beginning to color, about 5 minutes. Add the apples and sugar and fry gently for a further 3 minutes.

2 Add the mustard, pumpkin, and stock and bring just to a boil. Reduce the heat, cover with a lid, and simmer gently for about 20 minutes until the pumpkin and apples are very soft and falling apart.

3 Transfer to a food processor or blender and blend until smooth, or use a hand blender and blend the soup while still in the pan.

4 Stir in half the crème fraîche, season to taste with salt and pepper, and heat through gently. Ladle into soup bowls, spoon over the remaining crème fraîche, and serve sprinkled with pumpkin seeds.

serves 4–5

creamy pumpkin soup

preparation time: 10 minutes
cooking time: 25 minutes

- ⅓ cup olive oil
- 2 red onions, chopped
- 2 garlic cloves, chopped
- 2 tablespoons fresh ginger, chopped
- 2 lbs pumpkin, skinned, seeded, and cut into chunks
- 4½ cups chicken or vegetable stock
- ½ cup heavy cream
- salt and pepper

1 Heat the oil in a large, heavy-based saucepan. Add the onions and sauté gently for 3–4 minutes until softened. Add the garlic and ginger and sauté for another minute.

2 Add the pumpkin chunks and stock and bring to a boil. Reduce the heat, cover with a lid, and simmer very gently for 20 minutes until the pumpkin is beginning to fall apart.

3 Transfer to a food processor or blender and blend until smooth, or use a hand blender and blend the soup while still in the pan.

4 Stir in the cream and season to taste with salt and pepper. Reheat gently before serving.

serves 5–6

pumpkin and bean patties
with guacamole

preparation time: 30 minutes
cooking time: about 50 minutes

- 2 lbs pumpkin, seeded
- 1 x 15 oz can red kidney
  beans, drained and rinsed
- 1 tablespoon chopped fresh
  cilantro
- 1 small red onion, finely
  chopped
- 1 large egg
- 1 cup breadcrumbs

- vegetable or peanut oil, for
  frying

GUACAMOLE:

- 1 large ripe avocado
- 2 tomatoes, skinned
- 2 tablespoons lime juice
- 2 tablespoons sweet chile
  sauce
- salt and pepper

1 Cut the pumpkin into large wedges and put in a shallow baking dish. Season lightly and roast in a preheated oven at 400°F for about 40 minutes until just tender. Remove the skin.

2 Place the pumpkin flesh in a food processor and blend until broken into small pieces. Add the beans, cilantro, a generous half of the chopped onion, and salt and pepper to taste. Blend to a coarse paste. Add the egg and ½ cup of the breadcrumbs and blend quickly until just combined, so the mixture is still quite chunky.

3 Using tablespoons, divide the mixture into 8 pieces. Using your hands, shape each piece into a ball then flatten slightly into a cake. Turn the cakes in the remaining breadcrumbs until evenly coated.

4 To make the guacamole, halve and pit the avocado and scoop the flesh into a small bowl. Scoop the seeds out of the tomatoes and discard. Finely chop the flesh and add to the bowl. Mash lightly to make a chunky paste. Add the reserved onion, lime juice, chile sauce, and salt and pepper and stir well. Place in a small serving dish and chill until needed.

5 Heat a thin layer of oil in a large frying pan. Add the pumpkin patties and sauté gently for 2–3 minutes on each side until golden. Drain and serve with the guacamole.

serves 4

pumpkin and beet ravioli with fresh herb butter

preparation time: 30 minutes, plus chilling
cooking time: 5 minutes

- 2½ cups pasta flour
- 2 large eggs
- 3 large egg yolks
- 2 tablespoons olive oil
- ¼ teaspoon salt
- 9 oz pumpkin, seeded
- 1 small raw beet, about 3 oz
- 1 garlic clove, crushed

- beaten egg white, for glazing
- ½ oz bunch of fresh herbs
  (chives, parsley, tarragon)
- 1 stick (½ cup) unsalted butter
- 1 scallion, finely chopped
- finely grated zest of 1 lemon
  plus 2 teaspoons juice
- salt and pepper

cook's tip

Because these ravioli take a while to prepare it's well worth making them in advance. Once shaped, place them on a lightly floured tray or board and cover loosely. Chill for up to 8 hours before cooking.

1 To make the pasta, place the flour on a work surface and make a well in the middle. Break in the eggs, then add the egg yolks, the oil, and salt. Lightly whisk the eggs with a fork, gradually bringing in the flour. Once the flour is partly worked in use your fingers to mix the paste into a soft dough, adding a tablespoon of cold water if the dough feels dry. Once the dough is smooth and elastic, wrap in plastic wrap and chill for 30 minutes.

2 Cut the skin away from the pumpkin and finely grate the flesh into a bowl. Peel and finely grate the beet into the bowl. Add a little salt and pepper along with the garlic and mix until smooth.

3 Cut the pasta dough in half and roll out each half as thinly as possible on a floured surface, each to a 13-inch square.

4 Brush one square with the egg white. Place 25 teaspoons of the filling in five evenly spaced rows over the dough. Gently lay the second sheet of dough on top, pressing down firmly between each mound of filling. Use a sharp knife or pastry wheel to cut the ravioli into squares. Transfer to a lightly floured tray.

5 Discard any tough stalks from the herbs and chop finely. Melt the butter in a small pan and add the herbs, scallion, lemon zest and juice, and salt and pepper. Set aside.

6 Bring a large pan of salted water to a boil. Gently drop the ravioli into the pan and bring back to a boil. Cook for 3 minutes. Don't overcook the pasta or it will become soggy and fall apart. Drain and arrange on warm plates. Spoon over the herb butter and serve immediately.

serves 4

pumpkin oven fries with spicy salsa

preparation time: 10 minutes
cooking time: 30 minutes

- 3 lb wedge from a large
  pumpkin, seeded
- ⅓ cup olive oil
- 1 teaspoon mild chili powder

FOR THE SALSA:

- 7 oz cherry tomatoes
- 2 scallions

- 1 celery stick, finely chopped
- 4 tablespoons chopped fresh
  cilantro
- 4 tablespoons lime juice
- 2 teaspoons superfine sugar
- salt and pepper

1 Cut the pumpkin into thin wedges and then cut away the skin. Cut each wedge into fries, about ½-inch thick. Mix the oil with the chili powder and salt. Toss with the pumpkin pieces and place on a baking sheet, spreading out to an even layer. Roast in a preheated oven at 400°F for about 30 minutes, turning the fries frequently until golden and just tender.

2 Meanwhile make the salsa. Halve the tomatoes and discard the seeds, then chop the flesh. Trim and finely chop the scallions.

3 Mix together the tomatoes, scallions, celery, cilantro, lime juice, sugar, and salt and pepper. Transfer to a small bowl and serve as an accompaniment to the fries.

serves 4

roasted pumpkin and red pepper wraps

preparation time: 10 minutes
cooking time: about 45 minutes

- 2 red bell peppers, seeded
  and cored
- 1 lb pumpkin, seeded
- ¼ cup olive oil
- 3 oz mild, pickled sweet
  chiles, drained

- 2 large flour tortillas
- 3½ oz Gruyère cheese, grated
- ¼ cup sour cream
- salt and pepper

1 Cut the bell peppers into chunky wedges. Skin the pumpkin and slice very thinly. Put the peppers and pumpkin in a shallow baking dish and drizzle with the oil and a little salt and pepper. Roast in a preheated oven at 400°F for about 40 minutes until soft and lightly colored.

2 Thinly slice the chiles. Heat a large frying pan without any oil and lightly cook each tortilla for 30 seconds on each side. Place on a broiling rack and scatter with the pepper and pumpkin slices, then the chiles, cheese, and salt and pepper.

3 Cook under the broiler for 2–3 minutes until the cheese is melting. Spread with the sour cream and roll up. Serve warm.

serves 2

variation

For a more substantial snack add some thinly sliced cooked chicken with the pumpkin slices.

foil-roasted pumpkin wedges

preparation time: 10 minutes
cooking time: about 40 minutes

- small handful of fresh herbs
  (chives, parsley, oregano,
  basil)
- ½ cup pumpkin seed oil or
  olive oil
- ¼ cup lemon juice
- ½ teaspoon superfine sugar
- 2 garlic cloves, crushed
- 2–2½ lb whole pumpkin

1 Cut four 12-inch squares of aluminum foil.

2 Discard any tough stalks from the herbs and finely chop the leaves. Mix together with the oil, lemon juice, sugar, and garlic.

3 Halve the pumpkin and discard the seeds. Cut each half into four wedges. Put two wedges in each square of foil with the skin sides down. Spoon the dressing over them, then bring the foil up over the pumpkin and scrunch the edges together to seal completely. Roast in a preheated oven at 400°F for 25 minutes or until the pumpkin is almost tender, then open up the foil and roast for a further 10–15 minutes until lightly browned. Serve hot.

serves 4

pumpkin fritters with sour cream

preparation time: 10 minutes
cooking time: 5–10 minutes

- 1 cup all-purpose flour
- ½ teaspoon baking powder
- 1 large egg
- ⅔ cup cold water
- 2 lbs pumpkin, seeded
- ½ oz fresh herbs (parsley, rosemary, thyme)
- ⅔ cup sour cream
- oil for deep frying
- salt and pepper

1 Put the flour and baking powder in a mixing bowl. Make a well in the middle and add the egg. Measure out the cold water and pour a little into the well. Whisk together the egg and the water, gradually incorporating the flour to make a thick paste. Whisk in the remaining water to make a smooth batter.

2 Cut the pumpkin into ¾-inch thick wedges. Discard any tough stalks from the herbs. Chop the herbs finely and mix with the sour cream and a little salt and pepper. Transfer to a small serving dish.

3 Heat 2 inches of oil in a large, heavy-based saucepan until the oil sizzles when you spoon a little batter into it.

4 Dip each pumpkin wedge into the batter and carefully lower into the oil. Saute for 2–3 minutes until pale golden. Drain with a slotted spoon and place on a plate lined with paper towels while cooking the rest. Serve with the sour cream.

serves 4–6

prosciutto-wrapped pumpkin wedges

preparation time: 5 minutes
cooking time: 13 minutes

- 1¼ lbs pumpkin, seeded
- 6 wafer thin slices prosciutto,
  about 3 oz
- 1 teaspoon finely chopped
  fresh rosemary
- ¼ cup lemon juice
- ⅓ cup walnut oil
- salt and pepper

1 Cut the pumpkin into six even-sized wedges, then cut each wedge in half. Cut away the skin. Blanch the pumpkin pieces in boiling, lightly salted water for 4–5 minutes until just tender. Drain and cool slightly.

2 Cut each prosciutto slice in half lengthwise. Loosely wrap each one around a wedge of pumpkin and place on a rimmed baking sheet.

3 Mix together the rosemary, lemon juice, oil, and a little salt and pepper and spoon the dressing over the pumpkin. Bake in a preheated oven at 425°F for about 8 minutes until the prosciutto is just starting to color. Serve the wraps warm with any juices spooned over them.

serves 4

cook's tip

These little wraps make a great starter served on a bed of salad leaves, or you can make smaller ones for hors d'oeuvres.

pumpkin and pearl onions
in balsamic vinegar

preparation time: 10 minutes
cooking time: 50 minutes

- 1 lb pearl onions
- ⅓ cup olive oil
- 1½ lb wedge from a large
  pumpkin, seeded
- 2 tablespoons light brown
  sugar
- 2 bay leaves
- ⅓ cup raisins
- ½ cup balsamic vinegar
- salt and pepper

1 Peel the onions but leave them whole. Put them in a baking pan in which they line the base in a single layer. Pour the oil over them and roast in a preheated oven at 375°F for 20 minutes until they begin to soften.

2 Meanwhile, cut away the skin from the pumpkin and cut the flesh into 1-inch chunks. Add to the pan with the sugar, bay leaves, raisins, vinegar, and a little salt and pepper. Stir the ingredients together until combined.

3 Cover with a lid or foil and bake for 30 minutes until the onions and pumpkin are tender. Remove the bay leaves and serve the vegetables warm or cold with cheese or cold cuts.

serves 4

mashed pumpkin and potatoes
with garlic crème fraîche

preparation time: 8 minutes
cooking time: 20 minutes

- 1 lb large potatoes, cut into chunks
- 2 lbs pumpkin, seeded, peeled, and cut into chunks
- 3 garlic cloves, crushed
- ½ cup crème fraîche
- salt and pepper

1 Put the potatoes in a large saucepan, cover with cold water, and add a little salt. Bring to a boil. Add the pumpkin and cook for 15–20 minutes until the potatoes and pumpkin are very tender. Drain well and return to the pan.

2 Mash the vegetables thoroughly with a potato masher. Add the garlic, crème fraîche, and a little salt and pepper and mash until smooth. Serve hot.

serves 4

pumpkin and lentil dhal

preparation time: 5 minutes
cooking time: 20–25 minutes

- 1½ cups red split lentils
- 3¼ cups vegetable stock
- 1 small onion, finely chopped
- 2-inch piece of fresh ginger, finely chopped
- 2 garlic cloves, crushed
- ½ teaspoon ground turmeric
- 2 teaspoons cumin seeds, crushed
- 1¼ lbs pumpkin, seeded
- salt and pepper

1 Thoroughly wash the lentils in a sieve. Place in a large, heavy-based saucepan and add the stock, onion, ginger, garlic, and spices. Bring slowly to a boil.

2 Cover the pan and leave the mixture to simmer gently for 10 minutes until the lentils are just beginning to soften.

3 Meanwhile, cut away the skin from the pumpkin and cut the flesh into ½-inch cubes. Add to the pan. Cook for a further 5–8 minutes, stirring frequently, until the lentils are pulpy and thickened and the pumpkin is tender. Serve hot.

serves 4–6

cook's tip

A good dish to make in advance, this simple accompaniment tastes even better when reheated. It is delicious with any spicy food, or with a roasted chicken and a green salad.

lunch and dinner

pumpkin and couscous salad
with dried fruit

preparation time: 10 minutes
cooking time: 7 minutes

- 1 cup couscous
- 1¼ cups boiling water
- 1 lb wedge from a large
  pumpkin, seeded
- ⅓ cup olive oil
- ¼ cup pine nuts
- 1 teaspoon cumin seeds,
  lightly crushed

- 2 garlic cloves, thinly sliced
- 3 oz dried no-soak apricots or
  prunes, chopped
- ⅓ cup pumpkin seed oil
- ¼ cup lemon juice
- ½ oz bunch of mint and
  parsley
- salt and pepper

1 Put the couscous in a large bowl, add the water, and allow to stand while preparing the pumpkin.

2 Cut away the skin from the pumpkin. Cut the flesh into small chunks. Heat ¼ cup of the olive oil in a frying pan and sauté the pumpkin pieces for about 5 minutes, stirring frequently, until tender and lightly browned. Add the pine nuts, cumin seeds, and garlic and sauté for a further 1–2 minutes until the nuts are lightly colored. Allow to cool slightly.

3 Empty the contents of the pan into the couscous and add the remaining olive oil, the dried fruit, pumpkin seed oil, lemon juice, and salt and pepper. Chop the herbs, discarding any tough stalks, and add to the bowl. Toss the salad well. Cover and chill until ready to serve.

serves 5–6

pumpkin with feta and olives

preparation time: 10 minutes
cooking time: 7 minutes

- 1 lemon
- ½ cup extra virgin olive oil
- 14 oz pumpkin, seeded
- 1 teaspoon paprika

- 2 garlic cloves, thinly sliced
- 2 oz black olives
- 7 oz feta cheese, diced
- salt and pepper

1 Pare several strips of zest from the lemon using a sharp knife. Squeeze ¼ cup lemon juice and put it in a bowl with the pared zest, ¼ cup of the olive oil, and a little salt and pepper.

2 Cut the pumpkin into ¾-inch cubes. Put them on a plate and toss with the paprika and salt and pepper. Heat the remaining oil in a frying pan and gently sauté the pumpkin for about 5–6 minutes until just tender and lightly colored. Add the garlic slices and sauté for a further minute.

3 Empty the pumpkin and oil into the prepared dressing. Add the olives and cheese and toss together gently. Cover and chill until ready to serve.

serves 5–6

cook's tip

This quick and easy recipe makes a great tapas-style dish for serving before a hearty main course. Any leftovers can be chilled overnight.

crab and grilled pumpkin salad

preparation time: 15 minutes
cooking time: 10 minutes

- 13 oz wedge from a large
  pumpkin, seeded
- 3½ oz snow peas
- ½ bunch of scallions
- ¼ cucumber
- 3½ oz beansprouts
- ¼ cup pumpkin seeds
- ⅓ cup olive oil

- 2 garlic cloves, thinly sliced
- 1 small red chile, seeded and
  thinly sliced
- 2 teaspoons light brown
  sugar
- ¼ cup lime juice
- 7 oz white crabmeat
- salt

1 Remove the skin from the pumpkin and cut the flesh into ¼-inch thick slices. Cut them into more manageable size pieces if they are very large.

2 Shred the snow peas lengthwise. Trim and thinly slice the scallions. Cut the cucumber into matchsticks. Put the snow peas, scallions, cucumber, beansprouts, and pumpkin seeds into a large bowl.

3 Brush a grill pan with a little of the oil and grill the pumpkin slices, as many as you can fit at a time, until golden on each side, about 8–10 minutes. Drain and allow to cool.

4 To make the dressing, mix together the remaining oil, garlic, chile, sugar, lime juice, and a little salt. Scatter the pumpkin slices and crabmeat over the salad. Add the dressing and toss gently to serve.

serves 4

cook's tip

This salad is best served very fresh. You can prepare the vegetables and mix the dressing in advance, but toss the ingredients together right before serving.

spicy swordfish and pumpkin penne

preparation time: 5 minutes
cooking time: 12 minutes

- 2 swordfish steaks
- 2 tablespoons chile oil
- 10 oz pumpkin, seeded
- 6 oz penne pasta
- 2 tablespoons lime juice
- 1 teaspoon superfine sugar
- small handful of flat-leaf parsley
- salt

1 Pat the fish dry on paper towels and drizzle with 1 teaspoon of the oil and a little salt. Cut the pumpkin into ½-inch cubes, discarding the skin.

2 Heat the remaining oil in a frying pan. Add the pumpkin pieces and sauté gently, stirring frequently, for 5 minutes until browned and just tender. While the pumpkin is frying, bring a saucepan of water to a boil and cook the pasta until just tender.

3 Remove the pumpkin from the frying pan and set aside. Saute the fish for about 3 minutes on each side until cooked through. Using two forks break the fish into smaller pieces.

4 Drain the pasta and return to the saucepan. Add the fish, pumpkin, any cooking juices, lime juice, sugar, parsley, and a little salt. Toss the ingredients together and serve immediately.

serves 2

variation

Try using other firm-textured fish such as salmon or monkfish for this recipe.

pumpkin gnocchi with chile butter

preparation time: 20 minutes
cooking time: about 1 hour

- 2 lbs pumpkin
- 1 cup all-purpose flour
- 2 egg yolks
- several large sprigs of thyme
- 1 stick (½ cup) butter

- 1 red chile, seeded and thinly
  sliced
- 2 tablespoons lemon juice
- salt and pepper

1 If using a whole pumpkin, pierce it in several places with a knife; alternatively wrap a pumpkin wedge in foil. Bake in a preheated oven at 400°F for about 50 minutes until completely tender. Cool slightly then discard the seeds and skin and roughly chop the flesh.

2 Put the pumpkin flesh into a bowl and mash with a potato masher until smooth. Add the flour, egg yolks, and plenty of salt and pepper and beat until smooth.

3 Bring a large saucepan of salted water to a simmer. Remove the thyme from the sprigs and put it into a small pan with the butter, chile, lemon juice, and a little salt and pepper. Heat gently to melt the butter while cooking the gnocchi.

4 Take a tablespoonful of the gnocchi mixture and slide it into the pan of water with another spoon. Working quickly, add several more in the same way and cook until the gnocchi rise to the surface. Drain and place in a warm serving dish while cooking the rest in batches.

5 Spoon the chile butter over the gnocchi and serve hot.

serves 4–5

variation

Omit the chile and herbs and serve the gnocchi lavishly sprinkled with freshly grated Parmesan.

pumpkin, ricotta, and spinach tart

preparation time: 30 minutes, plus chilling
cooking time: 50 minutes

- 1¾ cups all-purpose flour
- 1 stick (½ cup) butter

FILLING:

- 14½ oz wedge from a large
  pumpkin, seeded
- ¼ stick (2 tablespoons) butter
- 1 onion, sliced

- 3 garlic cloves, sliced
- 3½ oz baby spinach leaves
- 3½ oz ricotta cheese
- 2 large eggs
- ⅔ cup light cream
- salt and pepper

1 To make the pastry, put the flour in a food processor with a little salt. Add the butter, cut into small pieces, and blend until the mixture resembles breadcrumbs. Add 1–2 teaspoons cold water and blend to a dough. Knead lightly until smooth then wrap in plastic wrap and chill for 30 minutes.

2 Roll out the pastry on a lightly floured surface and use to line a 9-inch, round, loose-based tart pan and trim off any excess. Line the pastry shell with parchment paper and fill with pie weights. Bake in a preheated oven at 400°F for 15 minutes then remove the weights and paper and cook for a further 5 minutes. Reduce the oven temperature to 350°F.

3 For the filling, cut away the skin from the pumpkin and cut the flesh into ¾-inch chunks. Melt the butter in a frying pan and sauté the onion, garlic, and pumpkin for 5 minutes until just beginning to color. Add the spinach to the pan and stir into the vegetables until it wilts slightly. Empty the vegetable mixture into the pastry shell and spread in an even layer to the edges.

4 Place spoonfuls of the ricotta over the filling. Beat the eggs with the cream and season with salt and pepper. Pour over the tart and bake for about 25 minutes until golden and lightly set. Serve warm or cold.

serves 4–6

roasted root vegetable and pumpkin tart

preparation time: 30 minutes
cooking time: 1 hour 10 minutes

- 1¼ lbs pumpkin, seeded
- 3 parsnips
- 3 carrots
- 2 red onions
- ¼ stick (2 tablespoons) butter
- 1 teaspoon superfine sugar
- ⅓ cup olive oil

- 2 tablespoons chopped fresh thyme
- 10 oz prepared pie pastry
- 2 tablespoons whole-grain mustard
- 2 tablespoons lemon juice
- salt and pepper

1 Cut the pumpkin into ¾-inch chunks, discarding the skin. Cut the parsnips and carrots lengthwise into quarters and then widthwise in half. Cut the onions into wedges.

2 Place all the vegetables in a large roasting pan. Add the butter, sugar, olive oil, and thyme. Season lightly with salt and pepper and roast in a preheated oven at 400°F for about 1 hour, tossing the ingredients once or twice during roasting, until golden.

3 Meanwhile, roll out the pastry and use to line a 9-inch loose-based tart pan. Line with parchment paper and pie weights. Put the pan in the oven under the vegetables and bake for 20 minutes. Remove the paper and weights and cook for a further 5 minutes or until golden.

4 When the vegetables are roasted, place half of them in a food processor and add the mustard, lemon juice, and salt and pepper. Blend until smooth.

5 Spread the puree over the pastry shell and pile the roasted vegetables on top. Return the tart to the oven for 10 minutes until heated through.

serves 6

cook's tip

Serve this tart as a light vegetarian dish or as an accompaniment to sausages or roast meat. It can be assembled several hours in advance and then reheated in a hot oven for 20–25 minutes.

goat cheese and pumpkin soufflé

preparation time: 15 minutes
cooking time: 35 minutes

- 8 oz pumpkin, seeded
- 3 tablespoons butter
- ¼ cup all-purpose flour
- ¾ cup plus 1 tablespoon milk
- ½ teaspoon mild chili powder

- 5 large eggs, separated
- 3½ oz firm goat cheese, crumbled
- salt

1 Finely grate the pumpkin, discarding the skin. Use 1 tablespoon of the butter to thoroughly grease a 6-cup soufflé mold.

2 Melt the remaining butter in a saucepan. Add the flour and cook, stirring, for 1 minute. Remove from the heat and gradually blend in the milk, stirring. Return to the heat and cook, stirring, until the sauce is very thick and bubbling. Cool slightly then add the chili powder, egg yolks, grated pumpkin, and goat cheese.

3 Whisk the egg whites in a large bowl until stiff peaks form. Using a large metal spoon, fold a quarter of the whites into the sauce to lighten it. Pour the mixture onto the remaining whites and fold in until evenly combined. Place in the prepared mold, smoothing down so that the top is level.

4 Bake in a preheated oven at 350°F for 30 minutes until well risen and golden. Serve immediately with a green salad.

serves 5–6

sweet potato, pancetta, and pumpkin stew

preparation time: 20 minutes
cooking time: 40 minutes

- 2 lb wedge from a large pumpkin, seeded
- 1 teaspoon mild chili powder
- 1 lb sweet potatoes, scrubbed
- 1 eggplant, about 10 oz
- ½ cup olive oil
- 3½ oz pancetta or bacon, diced
- 2 onions, chopped
- 4 garlic cloves, crushed
- 2 x 14 oz cans chopped tomatoes
- ¼ cup chopped fresh oregano
- ⅔ cup vegetable stock
- salt and pepper

1 Cut the pumpkin into large chunks, cutting away the skin. Toss the pieces in the chili powder. Cut the sweet potatoes into similar-size chunks. Cut the eggplant into small cubes.

2 Heat ¼ cup of the oil in a large, heavy-based saucepan. Add the pancetta and onions and sauté gently for 5 minutes until lightly browned. Add the eggplant and drizzle with the remaining oil. Cook gently for 5 minutes, stirring frequently.

3 Add the garlic, tomatoes, oregano, pumpkin, sweet potato, and stock to the pan. Bring to a boil. Reduce the heat, cover with a lid, and leave to simmer gently for about 30 minutes until the vegetables are tender but still retain their shape.

4 Check the seasoning and serve hot with rice, pasta, or whole-grain bread, or as an accompaniment to grilled sausages or barbecued meat.

serves 5–6

pumpkin, veal, and red bean goulash

preparation time: 25 minutes
cooking time: about 1¾ hours

- 2 lbs lean veal
- ⅓ cup olive oil
- 2 large onions, chopped
- 4 garlic cloves, sliced
- 4 tablespoons paprika
- small handful of oregano or rosemary sprigs
- 14 oz can chopped tomatoes
- 1¼ cups meat or vegetable stock
- 2 tablespoons dark brown sugar
- 1½ lbs pumpkin, seeded
- 15 oz can red kidney beans, rinsed and drained
- salt and pepper
- sour cream, to serve

1 Cut the meat into small cubes, discarding any excess fat. Toss the meat with a little salt and pepper.

2 Heat the oil in a large, heavy-based saucepan. Sauté half the meat for about 6–8 minutes until well browned. Remove with a slotted spoon then sauté the rest and remove. Sauté the onions for 5 minutes. Return the meat to the pan with the garlic, paprika, and herbs and cook for 1 minute.

3 Stir in the chopped tomatoes, stock, and sugar and bring slowly to a boil. Reduce the heat, cover with a lid, and simmer gently for about 1 hour until just tender.

4 Meanwhile, cut the pumpkin into small cubes, discarding the skin. Add to the pan with the red kidney beans. Cover and cook for 20–25 minutes until the pumpkin is tender, adding a little more stock if the stew starts to look dry. Serve in shallow dishes, swirled with sour cream.

serves 6

beef and pumpkin curry

preparation time: 25 minutes
cooking time: about 1½ hours

- ⅓ cup vegetable oil
- 1 red bell pepper, seeded and cut into chunks
- 1 green bell pepper, seeded and cut into chunks
- 2 onions, sliced
- 1 teaspoon ground turmeric
- 2 tablespoons coriander seeds, lightly crushed
- 2 teaspoons superfine sugar
- 1½ lbs lean stewing steak, cut into small chunks

- 3 garlic cloves, sliced
- 1 oz fresh ginger, chopped
- 1 red chile, seeded and chopped
- 14 oz can chopped tomatoes
- 2½ cups beef or chicken stock
- 2 lbs pumpkin, seeded
- salt
- crème fraîche, to serve

1 Heat the oil in a large, heavy-based saucepan. Add the bell peppers and sauté for 4–5 minutes until they start to color. Drain with a slotted spoon and set aside. Add the onions, turmeric, coriander, sugar, and beef and sauté gently for 5 minutes or until lightly colored.

2 Add the garlic, ginger, and chile to the pan and cook for 2 minutes, stirring. Add the tomatoes and stock and bring slowly to a boil. Reduce the heat, cover with a lid and simmer on the lowest heat for 1 hour until the beef is tender.

3 Meanwhile, cut away the skin from the pumpkin and cut the flesh into chunks. Add to the pan along with the red and green bell peppers. Cook gently for 20 minutes until the pumpkin is very soft. Season with salt if necessary and serve with crème fraîche and basmati rice.

serves 5–6

pumpkin, potato, and onion pie

preparation time: 20 minutes
cooking time: about 50 minutes

- 2 lbs large potatoes
- 2 lbs pumpkin, seeded
- 1 large onion, thinly sliced
- 3 garlic cloves, crushed
- 1¼ cups heavy cream

- ½ cup milk
- plenty of freshly grated
  nutmeg
- salt and pepper

1 Cut the potatoes into ⅛-inch thick slices. Cut away the skin from the pumpkin and cut the flesh into ⅛-inch thick slices. If the pumpkin slices are very long, cut them down so they are a similar size to the potatoes.

2 Bring a large saucepan of lightly salted water to a boil. Add the vegetables, return to a boil and cook for 2 minutes. Drain.

3 Arrange half the slices in a large, shallow baking dish. Scatter with the sliced onions, then with the remaining sliced vegetables. Mix the garlic with the cream, milk, and salt and pepper and pour over the vegetables. Grate plenty of nutmeg over the surface and bake in a preheated oven at 350°F for about 45 minutes until the vegetables are tender and the surface is golden.

serves 6

baked pumpkin with gruyère

preparation time: 10 minutes
cooking time: about 1 hour

- 2 small whole pumpkins, each about 5 inches in diameter
- 1½ lbs baking potatoes
- ¼ stick (2 tablespoons) butter
- 2 tablespoons whole-grain mustard
- 5 oz Gruyère cheese, grated
- salt and pepper

1 Pierce each pumpkin several times with the tip of a sharp knife. Bake in a preheated oven at 350°F for about 40 minutes until tender.

2 Meanwhile, cut the potatoes into large chunks and cook in boiling, salted water for about 20 minutes until tender. Drain and return to the pan.

3 Raise the oven temperature to 425°F. Halve the pumpkins vertically. Discard the seeds then scoop the flesh into the pan with the potatoes, reserving the pumpkin shells. Add the butter, mustard, half the cheese, and a little salt and pepper. Mash well using a potato masher until smooth.

4 Pile the mixture back into the pumpkin shells and place them in a shallow baking dish. Sprinkle with the remaining Gruyère and return to the oven for a further 15 minutes until the Gruyère is melting and beginning to color.

serves 4

sausage, pumpkin,
and sun-dried tomato risotto

preparation time: 15 minutes
cooking time: 35 minutes

- 1 lb pumpkin, seeded
- 2 oz sun-dried tomatoes in oil
- 3¾ cups hot chicken or
  vegetable stock
- 2 tablespoons olive oil
- 1 lb garlic and herb pork
  sausages

- ½ stick (¼ cup) butter
- 1 large onion, chopped
- 1¼ cups Italian risotto rice
- ½ cup freshly grated
  Parmesan cheese
- salt and pepper

1 Cut away the skin from the pumpkin and coarsely grate the flesh.

2 Thinly slice the sun-dried tomatoes and put them in a large measuring cup with the hot stock. Heat the oil in a large, heavy-based saucepan. Add the sausages and sauté gently on all sides until browned, about 8 minutes. Remove from the pan and cut into diagonal slices.

3 Add half the butter and the onion to the pan and sauté gently for 3–4 minutes until softened. Add the rice and cook for 1 minute, stirring. Pour in a little of the stock and cook until it has evaporated.

4 Pour in a little more stock and cook, stirring, until it is absorbed. Continue cooking, gradually adding the remaining stock and stirring frequently until the risotto is thick and creamy but the grains retain a little texture. This will take 15–20 minutes.

5 Return the sausages to the pan with the grated pumpkin, the remaining butter, and half the Parmesan. Cook gently for 2 minutes, stirring.

6 Check the risotto for seasoning then transfer to plates, and serve scattered with the remaining Parmesan.

serves 4

pumpkin and pine nut risotto

preparation time: 20 minutes
cooking time: about 35 minutes

- 1 lb pumpkin, seeded
- 3 tablespoons butter
- 2 tablespoons olive oil
- ½ cup pine nuts
- 1 onion, chopped
- 2 garlic cloves, crushed
- 1⅛ cups Italian risotto rice

- ⅔ cup white wine
- 3¾ cups hot chicken or
  vegetable stock
- ½ cup freshly grated
  Parmesan cheese
- salt and pepper

1 Cut away the skin from the pumpkin and cut the flesh into ¾-inch chunks. Melt half the butter in a large, heavy-based saucepan with the oil and sauté the pumpkin for 3 minutes. Add the pine nuts and sauté for 2 minutes until pale golden. Drain with a slotted spoon and set aside.

2 Add the onion to the pan and sauté for 3–4 minutes until very soft. Add the garlic and rice and cook, stirring, for 1 minute. Pour in the wine and let it bubble until evaporated.

3 Add a little of the hot stock and cook, stirring, until it is absorbed. Add a little more stock and cook until absorbed. Continue cooking, gradually adding the remaining stock, for about 20 minutes, stirring until the risotto is thick and creamy but the grains retain a little texture. You might not need all the stock.

4 Return the pumpkin and the pine nuts to the pan with the remaining butter and half the Parmesan. Check the seasoning and spoon the risotto onto plates. Serve sprinkled with the remaining Parmesan.

serves 4–5

moroccan pumpkin and lamb couscous

preparation time: 25 minutes
cooking time: 1¼ hours

- 1½ lbs pumpkin, seeded
- 14 oz lean lamb (fillet or leg)
- ⅓ cup olive oil
- 1 large onion, chopped
- 1 teaspoon ground turmeric
- ½ teaspoon hot chili powder
- 1-inch piece fresh ginger, grated
- 1 cinnamon stick
- 3 garlic cloves, sliced
- 2 large carrots, sliced
- 2½ cups lamb or vegetable stock
- 15 oz can chickpeas, rinsed and drained
- 1⅓ cups couscous
- small handful of cilantro, chopped
- salt and pepper

1 Cut the pumpkin into chunky wedges and cut away the skin. Chop the flesh into small chunks. Trim any excess fat from the lamb and season lightly with salt and pepper.

2 Heat the oil in a large heavy-based saucepan. Add the onion and sauté gently for 3 minutes. Add the lamb and sauté for about 5 minutes until it starts to color. Stir in the spices, garlic, and carrots and sauté for 2 minutes.

3 Add the stock and bring slowly to a boil. Reduce the heat, cover with a lid, and simmer on the lowest possible heat for about 50 minutes until the lamb is tender.

4 Stir in the chickpeas and pumpkin and cook gently for 15 minutes until the pumpkin is tender, adding a little water if the stew starts to dry out.

5 While the pumpkin is cooking, put the couscous in a heatproof bowl and cover with boiling water. Cover with foil or a plate and leave for 5 minutes until the water has been absorbed. Lightly season the couscous with salt and pepper and fluff up with a fork.

6 Stir the cilantro into the stew, check the seasoning and remove the cinnamon stick. Serve the stew spooned over the couscous.

serves 4–5

pumpkin and leek phyllo strudel

preparation time: 30 minutes
cooking time: 45–50 minutes

- 1¼ lbs pumpkin, seeded
- ¾ stick (6 tablespoons) butter
- ¾ cup coarse breadcrumbs
- 3 small leeks, sliced
- 7 oz mushrooms, sliced
- ½ cup crème fraîche

- 2 teaspoons hot horseradish
  sauce
- 4 oz phyllo pastry
- pumpkin seeds, to sprinkle
- salt and pepper

1 Cut the pumpkin into ½-inch cubes, discarding the skin. Melt 2 tablespoons of the butter in a frying pan and sauté the breadcrumbs for 3–4 minutes until crisp and golden. Remove with a slotted spoon and set aside on a plate.

2 Melt another 2 tablespoons of the butter and sauté the leeks and mushrooms for 5 minutes, stirring frequently, until golden. Transfer to a bowl and mix with the chopped pumpkin and salt and pepper.

3 Combine the crème fraîche and horseradish. Melt the remaining butter. Lay two or three sheets of phyllo (depending on size) on a work surface, overlapping the edges slightly, to make an 18 x 12-inch rectangle. Brush with a little of the butter and cover with a second layer of phyllo pastry, arranging them differently so the edges are not all in the same place. Brush with more butter and cover with a final layer of phyllo.

4 Spread the pumpkin mixture over the pastry, to within about 2 inches of the edges. Scatter with the breadcrumbs and then spoon the crème fraîche along the middle. Fold the short ends of the pastry over the filling, then roll up from one of the long sides. Carefully transfer the strudel, with the seam underneath, to a lightly greased baking sheet.

5 Brush the strudel with any remaining butter and sprinkle with the pumpkin seeds. Bake for 35–40 minutes until the pastry is a deep golden brown and crisp. Leave to cool slightly before slicing and serving.

serves 4

smoked bacon, pumpkin, and cabbage stir-fry

preparation time: 8 minutes
cooking time: 12–15 minutes

- 14 oz pumpkin, seeded
- 1 lb green cabbage
- ¼ cup vegetable oil
- 2 tablespoons sesame oil
- 1 oz fresh ginger, finely chopped
- 4 garlic cloves, sliced
- 3½ oz smoked bacon, chopped
- ¼ cup pumpkin seeds
- soy sauce, to serve

1 Cut away the skin from the pumpkin and cut the flesh into small cubes. Discard the core from the cabbage and coarsely shred the leaves.

2 Heat the vegetable and sesame oils in a large frying pan or wok. Add the pumpkin and sauté gently for 5 minutes until just tender. Remove with a slotted spoon.

3 Add the ginger, garlic, bacon, and pumpkin seeds to the pan and sauté, stirring, for 2 minutes. Remove with a slotted spoon and set aside with the pumpkin.

4 Add the cabbage to the pan, adding a little extra oil if necessary, and stir-fry for 4–5 minutes until the cabbage is softened and lightly browned. Return the pumpkin and the bacon mixture to the pan and stir the ingredients together for 1 minute. Serve drizzled with a little soy sauce.

serves 4

chicken with black beans
and pumpkin mash

preparation time: 20 minutes
cooking time: 1¼ hours

- 2½ lbs pumpkin, seeded
- 4 chicken drumsticks
- 4 chicken thighs
- 1 teaspoon ground paprika
- ⅓ cup olive oil
- 2 onions, chopped
- 2 celery sticks, sliced
- 2 oz Spanish chorizo
  sausage, diced
- 2 cups chicken stock
- 15 oz can black beans
- 1 teaspoon dried oregano
- salt

1 Cut away the skin from the pumpkin. Cut a quarter of the pumpkin into large matchstick-sized fries. Roughly chop the rest. Toss all the chicken pieces in the paprika.

2 Heat the oil in a large, heavy-based frying pan and sauté the pumpkin fries for about 5 minutes until golden. Remove with a slotted spoon. Add the chicken pieces to the pan and sauté for about 5 minutes until golden, turning frequently, then remove with a slotted spoon and add the onions, celery, and sausage to the pan. Sauté gently for 5 minutes.

3 Put the chicken and onion mixture into an ovenproof casserole. Add the stock to the frying pan with the beans and oregano and bring to a boil. Pour over the chicken and cover with a lid. Bake in a preheated oven at 350°F for about 1 hour until the chicken is cooked through.

4 Meanwhile, cook the remaining pumpkin in boiling, lightly salted water for 12–15 minutes until tender. Drain well, then return to the pan and mash. Stir the pumpkin fries into the casserole. Serve the chicken hot with the mashed pumpkin.

serves 4

gingered noodles with cilantro and pumpkin wedges

preparation time: 10 minutes
cooking time: 6 minutes

- 1 lb pumpkin, seeded
- 2 tablespoons peanut or vegetable oil
- 4 oz rice stick noodles
- 1 oz fresh ginger, grated
- ½ oz fresh cilantro
- ¾ cup coconut milk
- 2 teaspoons Thai fish sauce
- salt

1 Cut the pumpkin into small cubes, discarding the skin. Heat the oil in a frying pan and sauté the pumpkin for about 5 minutes, stirring frequently, until lightly browned and tender.

2 Meanwhile, put the rice noodles in a large heatproof bowl, cover with boiling water, and leave for 4 minutes. Drain.

3 Add the ginger, cilantro, coconut milk, fish sauce, and a little salt to the pumpkin and heat through for 1 minute. Stir in the noodles until all the ingredients are thoroughly mixed together and serve immediately.

serves 2

variation

This makes a quick, easy and surprisingly rich supper dish. If desired, sauté some thinly sliced chicken before frying the pumpkin or add some cooked shrimp with the coconut milk.

chicken in a pumpkin shell

preparation time: 30 minutes
cooking time: about 1½ hours

- 1 whole pumpkin, about 10–11 inches in diameter
- 6 skinned, boneless chicken breasts
- ½ cup all-purpose flour
- ¼ stick (2 tablespoons) butter
- 2 tablespoons olive oil
- 2 large onions, chopped
- 13 oz zucchini, thinly sliced
- 3 red bell peppers, seeded and sliced
- 4 garlic cloves, crushed
- ½ teaspoon saffron strands, crumbled
- 14 oz can coconut milk
- ⅔ cup chicken or vegetable stock
- 1 cinnamon stick, halved
- 2 tablespoons cardamom pods
- salt and pepper

cook's tips

This dish makes a novel idea for a Halloween party or any other celebration. Once you've ladled out the chicken mixture you can easily scoop out the pumpkin from the shell. Serve with chunky, warm bread to complete the meal.

When preparing the pumpkin for baking, keep the piercing near the top, otherwise the liquid might seep out when you serve the dish.

1 Pierce the pumpkin all around the top with a skewer. Bake in a preheated oven at 375°F for about 1 hour until the flesh feels quite tender when the top of the pumpkin is pierced with a knife.

2 Meanwhile, chop the chicken into small pieces. Season the flour with salt and pepper and use to coat the chicken. Melt the butter with the oil in a large heavy-based saucepan and sauté the chicken, in batches if necessary, until golden. Remove with a slotted spoon.

3 Add the onions, zucchini, and red bell peppers to the pan and sauté gently for 5 minutes, adding a little extra oil if necessary. Return the chicken to the pan with the garlic, saffron, coconut milk, stock, and spices. Bring to a boil, then reduce the heat, cover, and simmer gently on the lowest possible heat for 1 hour.

4 Cut out a lid from the cooked pumpkin and remove it carefully, because it will be very hot inside. Scoop out and discard the seeds. Season the chicken to taste with salt and pepper and ladle into the pumpkin shell to serve. Alternatively, put it back in a low oven for up to 1 hour until ready to serve.

serves 6

maple roast ham with crushed pumpkin

preparation time: 20 minutes, plus soaking
cooking time: about 1 ½ hours

- 2 lb piece country-cured ham
- 2 onions, halved
- 2 carrots, roughly sliced
- 2 celery sticks, roughly sliced
- 3 bay leaves
- 2½ lb wedge from a large
  pumpkin, seeded

- ¼ stick (2 tablespoons)
  butter, melted
- ¾ cup maple syrup
- juice of 1 orange
- salt and pepper

cook's tip

If your broiler is in the oven, wait until the ham is cooked
and then keep it warm, covered with foil, while
browning the pumpkin.

1 Soak the ham overnight in plenty of cold water. Drain and
place in a deep, heavy-based saucepan. Tuck the onions,
carrots, celery, and bay leaves around the ham and season
with pepper. Add enough cold water to just cover the meat.
Bring slowly to a boil, reduce the heat, and simmer very gently,
covered, for 1 hour.

2 Meanwhile, cut the pumpkin into large pieces, discarding
the skin. Cook in a saucepan of boiling, salted water for 10–12
minutes until just tender. Drain and return to the pan. Lightly
butter a shallow baking dish. Preheat the oven to 400°F.

3 Lightly crush the pumpkin pieces by pushing them against
the side of the pan until they are broken up but not mashed.
Transfer to the buttered dish, spreading in an even layer.
Drizzle with the melted butter and plenty of salt and pepper.

4 When the ham is cooked, drain it, discarding the
vegetables, and cut away the skin. Place in a shallow baking
dish or small roasting pan with the skinned side up. Brush the
fat with maple syrup and pour the orange juice into the dish.

5 Bake for about 25 minutes, basting frequently with the
maple syrup and orange juice until pale golden brown. When
the ham is almost baked, broil the pumpkin for 5 minutes until
it begins to brown. Thinly slice the meat onto plates, spoon
any pan juices over it, and serve with the pumpkin.

serves 4

baking

pumpkin and orange drizzle cake

preparation time: 20 minutes
cooking time: about 1 hour

- 13 oz pumpkin, seeded
- 1½ sticks (¾ cup) unsalted
  butter, softened
- ¾ cup light brown sugar
- 3 eggs
- 1¾ cups self-rising flour
- 1 teaspoon baking powder

- ¼ cup ground almonds
- finely grated zest and juice of
  ½ small orange
- finely grated zest and juice of
  1 lemon
- ⅓ cup superfine sugar

1 Grease and line an 8-inch round cake pan. Cut the pumpkin into small pieces, discarding the skin. Steam over a pan of gently simmering water for about 20 minutes until just tender. Remove from the pan and blend in a food processor or blender to a smooth puree. Allow to cool.

2 Put the butter, sugar, eggs, flour, baking powder, ground almonds, orange zest, and lemon zest in a large mixing bowl and beat with a hand-held electric mixer until smooth. Stir in the pumpkin puree.

3 Transfer the mixture to the pan and level the surface. Bake the cake in a preheated oven at 350°F for about 40 minutes until risen and just firm to the touch. Allow to cool in the pan.

4 Mix together the orange juice, lemon juice, and sugar and spoon over the surface of the cake so the juice seeps into the cake and the sugar forms a crust.

serves 12

sweet pumpkin cake
with ricotta and lemon frosting

preparation time: 20 minutes
cooking time: about 1 hour

- 10 oz pumpkin, seeded
- 1½ sticks (¾ cup) unsalted butter, softened
- ¾ cup superfine sugar
- 1½ cups self-rising flour
- 1 teaspoon baking powder
- ½ teaspoon ground allspice
- 3 eggs

- ⅓ cup ground almonds
- ½ cup golden raisins

FROSTING:
- 5 oz ricotta cheese
- finely grated zest of 1 lemon, plus 2 teaspoons juice
- 1¾ cups confectioner's sugar

cook's tip _____

This recipe makes an interesting variation on carrot cake, with grated pumpkin taking the place of the more familiar carrots. The ricotta frosting provides a lovely, fresh tangy contrast to the cake but can be omitted for a simpler cake.

1 Grease and line a 7-inch square or 8-inch round cake pan. Cut away the skin from the pumpkin and finely grate the flesh.

2 Put the butter, sugar, flour, baking powder, allspice, eggs, and ground almonds in a large mixing bowl and beat with a hand-held electric mixer for about 2 minutes until creamy and smooth. Stir in the grated pumpkin and golden raisins until evenly mixed.

3 Pour the mixture into the pan and level the surface. Bake in a preheated oven at 325°F for about 1 hour or until risen and golden and the surface feels just firm. Leave the cake in the pan for 5 minutes then transfer to a wire rack to cool.

4 For the frosting, press the ricotta cheese through a sieve to remove the lumps. Add the lemon zest and juice and confectioner's sugar and stir until the mixture has a smooth consistency. Spread over the top of the cake with an offset spatula. Store in a cool place.

serves 12

chocolate and pumpkin seed brownies

preparation time: 15 minutes
cooking time: 35 minutes

- 7 oz vanilla fudge
- 10 oz semisweet chocolate
- 1¾ sticks (¾ cup plus 2 tablespoons) unsalted butter
- 3 eggs
- ½ cup superfine sugar
- ¾ cup self-rising flour
- ¾ cup pumpkin seeds

cook's tip

When baked, the brownie surface should still feel quite soft because of the high sugar content. Don't be tempted to cook them for longer as this will spoil the texture of the brownies.

1 Grease and line an 11 x 8-inch shallow baking pan. Chop the fudge into small pieces and set aside. Break the chocolate into a bowl and add the butter. Melt until smooth.

2 Beat together the eggs and the sugar. Beat in the melted chocolate mixture then stir in the flour and all but ¼ cup of the pumpkin seeds. Stir in the chopped fudge and pour into the pan, spreading it into the corners. Sprinkle with the reserved seeds.

3 Bake in a preheated oven at 375°F for about 35 minutes until the center feels just slightly firm. Leave to cool in the pan then transfer to a board and cut into small squares.

makes 15

layered pumpkin and banana teabread

preparation time: 20 minutes
cooking time: about 1¼ hours

- 8 oz pumpkin, seeded
- finely grated zest and juice of ½ lemon
- ¼ cup clear honey
- 2 small ripe bananas
- ¾ cup superfine sugar
- 1½ sticks (¾ cup) unsalted butter, softened
- 3 eggs
- 2¼ cups self-rising flour
- 1 teaspoon baking powder
- extra honey, for glazing

1 Grease and line a 2 lb loaf pan. Cut away the skin from the pumpkin and dice the flesh. Cook in a little boiling water for about 5 minutes or until tender. Drain the pumpkin and return to the pan. Mash with a potato masher until smooth. Stir in the lemon zest and juice and the honey.

2 Mash the bananas. Put the sugar, butter, eggs, flour, and baking powder into a mixing bowl and beat with a hand-held electric mixer for 2 minutes or until smooth. Stir in the bananas.

3 Spoon a third of the banana mixture into the pan and level the surface. Spread with half the pumpkin mixture. Spoon half the remaining banana mixture on top then spread with the remaining pumpkin mixture. Finally add the remaining banana mixture and level the surface.

4 Bake for 1¼ hours or until risen and firm to the touch. Leave in the pan for 10 minutes then transfer to a wire rack to cool. Drizzle the top of the cake with extra honey.

serves 10

seeded pumpkin bread

preparation time: 20 minutes, plus proofing
cooking time: 35–40 minutes

- 13 oz pumpkin, seeded
- 5 cups white bread flour
- 1 teaspoon salt
- ½ teaspoon ground mixed spice
- 2 tablespoons light brown sugar
- 2 teaspoons dry yeast
- ⅔ cup milk
- pumpkin seeds, for sprinkling

cook's tip

This golden, moist-textured bread is delicious served fresh with butter or accompanying soups and warming casseroles. It's also good toasted for breakfast.

1 Cut the pumpkin into small chunks, discarding the skin. Steam over a pan of simmering water until tender. Transfer to a food processor or blender and blend to a smooth puree.

2 Put the flour, salt, spice, sugar, and yeast into a large mixing bowl. Add the pumpkin puree and milk and mix to a smooth dough, using a round-bladed knife. If the dough feels a bit dry, add a dash more milk.

3 Turn out the dough onto a lightly floured surface and knead gently for about 10 minutes until the dough is smooth and elastic. Transfer to a lightly oiled bowl, cover with plastic wrap and leave to rise in a warm place until doubled in size, about 1 hour.

4 Lightly grease a large baking sheet. Turn out the dough onto a lightly floured surface and punch to deflate. Form loosely into an oval shape and transfer to the baking sheet. Cover with plastic wrap and leave to rise again until doubled in size.

5 Lightly brush the top of the bread with a little milk. Using a sharp knife, make several diagonal scores across the bread then sprinkle with the pumpkin seeds. Bake in a preheated oven at 400°F for 35–40 minutes until deep golden brown and the base sounds hollow when tapped. Cool on a wire rack.

makes 1 loaf

pumpkin and oatmeal rolls

preparation time: 20 minutes, plus proofing
cooking time: 15–20 minutes

- 13 oz pumpkin, seeded
- 4 cups white bread flour
- ½ cup medium-cut oatmeal
- 1 teaspoon salt
- 3 oz no-soak prunes, chopped
- 2 teaspoons superfine sugar
- 2 teaspoons dry yeast
- 1½ cups warm milk
- extra oatmeal, to sprinkle

1 Cut the pumpkin into very small cubes, discarding the skin. Put the flour, oatmeal, salt, prunes, sugar, yeast, and chopped pumpkin into a large mixing bowl. Add the milk to the bowl and stir with a round-bladed knife to make a soft dough, adding a dash more milk if the dough feels dry.

2 Turn out the dough onto a floured surface and knead for about 10 minutes until it is smooth and elastic. Transfer to a lightly oiled bowl, cover with plastic wrap and leave to rise in a warm place for about 1 hour until the dough has doubled in size.

3 Grease a large baking sheet. Turn out the dough onto a floured surface and punch to deflate. Cut into 8 even-sized pieces. Shape each piece into a round and place the rounds, well apart, on the baking sheet. Cover loosely with oiled plastic wrap and leave in a warm place for about 40 minutes until doubled in size.

4 Brush the tops of the rolls with a little milk and sprinkle with oatmeal. Bake in a preheated oven at 425°F for 15–20 minutes until risen and golden. Transfer to a wire rack to cool.

makes 8

bacon and pumpkin muffins

preparation time: 15 minutes
cooking time: 30 minutes

- ¼ cup olive oil
- 1 large onion, finely chopped
- 4 oz smoked bacon, diced
- 10 oz pumpkin, seeded
- 2 cups self-rising flour
- ½ cup cornmeal or fine polenta
- 2 teaspoons baking powder
- 3 eggs
- 1 cup milk

1 Line a 12-cup muffin pan with paper muffin cups.

2 Heat the oil in a frying pan and sauté the onion and bacon for 5 minutes until lightly browned. Cut away the skin from the pumpkin and finely grate the flesh.

3 Sift the flour, cornmeal, and baking powder into a large mixing bowl. Stir in the onion, bacon, and grated pumpkin. Beat the eggs with the milk and add to the bowl. Mix until just combined.

4 Divide the mixture among the paper cups and bake in a preheated oven at 400°F for 20–25 minutes or until risen, golden, and just firm. Transfer to a wire rack to cool. Serve buttered.

makes 12

variation

Omit the bacon and add ½ teaspoon chili powder when sifting the dry ingredients.

pumpkin, yogurt, and honey muffins

preparation time: 15 minutes
cooking time: 20–25 minutes

- 10 oz pumpkin, seeded
- 2 cups self-rising flour
- 2 teaspoons baking powder
- 1 teaspoon ground ginger

- ⅓ cup clear honey
- ½ stick (¼ cup) butter, melted
- ⅔ cup plain yogurt
- 3 eggs

1 Line a 12-cup muffin pan with paper muffin cups. Cut away the skin from the pumpkin and coarsely grate the flesh.

2 Sift the flour, baking powder, and ginger into a large mixing bowl. Stir in the grated pumpkin. Combine the honey, butter, yogurt, and eggs and add to the bowl. Mix until just combined.

3 Divide the mixture among the paper cups and bake in a preheated oven at 400°F for 20–25 minutes or until risen, golden, and just firm. Transfer to a wire rack to cool.

makes 12

white chocolate chip
and pumpkin cookies

preparation time: 15 minutes
cooking time: 20–25 minutes

- 8 oz pumpkin, seeded
- 1 stick (½ cup) unsalted
  butter, softened
- ½ cup superfine sugar
- 1 egg
- 1¼ cups old-fashioned
  oatmeal
- 1 cup self-rising flour

- 3½ oz white chocolate chips
- confectioner's sugar for
  dusting

1 Grease two baking sheets. Cut away the skin from the pumpkin and finely grate the flesh.

2 Beat together the butter and sugar until creamy. Beat in the grated pumpkin, then the egg, oatmeal, flour, and chocolate chips.

3 Place teaspoonfuls of the mixture on the baking sheets and flatten them slightly with the back of a spoon. Bake in a preheated oven at 350°F for about 20–25 minutes until risen and pale golden. Leave on the baking sheets for 2 minutes then transfer to a wire rack to cool. Dust lightly with the confectioner's sugar.

makes about 25

variation

Use semisweet or milk chocolate chips instead of the white ones. Alternatively, chop a bar of chocolate into small pieces and use instead of the chocolate chips.

decorated pumpkin cookies

preparation time: 25 minutes, plus chilling and decorating
cooking time: 15–20 minutes

- ½ small pumpkin, about ½ pound, seeded
- 3 cups all-purpose flour
- 1 teaspoon ground ginger
- ½ teaspoon grated nutmeg
- ¾ cup plus 2 tablespoons unsalted butter
- ¾ cup confectioner's sugar
- 2 egg yolks
- colored royal icing to decorate

1 Slice the pumpkin into wedges and cut away the skin. Finely grate the flesh.

2 Cut the butter into small pieces and put into a food processor with the flour, ginger, and nutmeg. Blend until the mixture resembles fine breadcrumbs. Add the grated pumpkin and confectioner's sugar and blend briefly until combined. Finally, add the egg yolks and blend to form a soft dough. Wrap the dough in plastic wrap and chill for at least 2 hours.

3 Lightly grease two baking sheets. Roll out the dough on a lightly floured surface and, using shaped cutters, cut out your cookies. Alternatively, you could create your own designs by making paper templates, placing them on top of the dough and then cutting round them with a knife.

4 Place the cookies slightly apart on the baking sheets and bake in a preheated oven at 350°F for 15–20 minutes, until golden. Transfer to a wire rack to cool.

5 Decorate the cookies with different colored royal icing. Spoon some colored icing into a piping bag with a writing nozzle. Pipe around the edges of the cookies, then leave to dry. Fill in with the same colored icing using a larger nozzle on the piping bag. Allow to dry, then decorate the cookies with patterns of your choice. Leave to set for 1 hour before serving.

makes 12

cook's tip

Because of the high sugar content of cookies, they will still be soft when they come out of the oven, so don't be tempted to bake them for longer. They will gradually harden as they cool on the wire rack.

desserts and
sweet treats

classic pumpkin pie

preparation time: 20 minutes
cooking time: 1 hour 10 minutes

- 10 oz prepared pie pastry
- 2 lbs pumpkin, seeded
- ⅔ cup light brown sugar
- 2 pieces crystallized ginger
  from a jar, chopped
- 1 teaspoon ground cinnamon
- 2 eggs, beaten
- ⅔ cup heavy cream
- confectioner's sugar, for
  dusting

1 Roll out the pastry on a lightly floured surface and use to line a 10-inch round, loose-based tart pan with a depth of 1½ inches. Line with parchment paper and pie weights and bake in a preheated oven at 400°F for 15 minutes. Remove the paper and weights and bake for a further 5 minutes. Reduce the oven temperature to 350°F.

2 Cut away the skin from the pumpkin and roughly chop the flesh. Steam over a pan of gently simmering water for about 20 minutes until just tender. Remove from the heat and allow to cool slightly.

3 Place the pumpkin flesh in a food processor or blender and add the sugar, ginger, cinnamon, and eggs. Blend to a smooth puree. Place the puree in a bowl and stir in the cream. Carefully pour into the pastry shell and bake for 30 minutes or until the pie is still slightly wobbly in the middle. Dust with confectioner's sugar and serve warm or cold with heavy cream.

serves 10

variation

Stir a little orange liqueur or brandy into some lightly whipped cream as an accompaniment.

cook's tip

To give your pie that extra special touch, cut out leaves from any left-over pastry and place around the top edge of the pie. These can be cooked at the same time as the pie on a separate baking sheet for 10 minutes, or until golden brown.

pumpkin amaretti cheesecake

preparation time: 20 minutes, plus chilling
cooking time: 35–40 minutes

- 7 oz amaretti or almond
  macaroons
- 3 tablespoons unsalted butter
- 14 oz pumpkin, seeded
- 14 oz regular cream cheese
- ⅓ cup superfine sugar
- 2 eggs
- 2 teaspoons vanilla extract
- ⅔ cup heavy cream
- ½ cup golden raisins

variation

The golden raisins add pockets of sweetness that combine perfectly with the pumpkin. For a nutty flavor, substitute ½ cup roughly chopped walnuts or pecans.

1 Grease and line the sides of a 7-inch springform pan with a strip of baking parchment.

2 Break 3 oz of the cookies into chunky pieces. Put the remainder in a plastic bag and crush them with a rolling pin. Melt the butter and stir in the crushed cookies until coated. Put the crushed cookies in the springform pan and press down in an even layer.

3 Cut away the skin from the pumpkin and finely grate the flesh. Beat the cream cheese in a bowl to soften it, then beat in the sugar, eggs, vanilla extract, and cream. Add the grated pumpkin, golden raisins, and broken cookies and stir until evenly mixed.

4 Pour the mixture onto the cookie base. Bake in a preheated oven at 325°F for 35–40 minutes until the center of the cheesecake feels just set. Allow to cool in the pan. Then chill until ready to serve.

serves 8

rhubarb, ginger, and pumpkin crumble

preparation time: 15 minutes
cooking time: 35 minutes

- 1¼ lbs pumpkin, seeded
- 13 oz rhubarb
- ½ cup light brown sugar
- 2 pieces crystallized ginger
  from a jar, plus ⅓ cup of
  the syrup

TOPPING:
- 1 cup all-purpose flour
- ½ cup ground almonds
- 1 stick (½ cup) unsalted butter
- ¼ cup light brown sugar
- whipped cream, for serving

1 Cut the pumpkin into small chunks, discarding the skin. Trim the rhubarb and cut it into 1-inch lengths. Put the pumpkin and rhubarb into a saucepan with the sugar and heat gently for 4–5 minutes until the rhubarb juices start to run.

2 Thinly slice the ginger and add with the syrup to the pan. Place in a shallow baking dish.

3 To make the topping, put the flour and almonds in a food processor. Add the butter, cut into small pieces, and blend until the mixture resembles breadcrumbs. Add the sugar and blend in until the mixture starts to cling together slightly. Empty the mixture over the pumpkin and rhubarb and spread it to the edges of the dish.

4 Bake in a preheated oven at 400°F for about 30 minutes until the crumble is golden. Serve with whipped cream.

serves 5–6

pumpkin meringue pie

preparation time: 30 minutes
cooking time: 45 minutes

- 8 oz prepared pie pastry
- 1½ lbs pumpkin, seeded
- juice of 3 large oranges, plus
  the finely grated zest of one
- ⅓ cup lemon juice

- ⅓ cup cornstarch
- ¾ cup water
- 1 cup, plus 2 tablespoons
  superfine sugar
- 3 egg whites

1 Roll out the pastry on a lightly floured surface and use to line a 9-inch round, loose-based tart pan with a depth of 1 inch. Line with parchment paper and pie weights and bake in a preheated oven at 400°F for 15 minutes. Remove the paper and weights and bake for a further 5 minutes until golden.

2 Meanwhile, remove the skin from the pumpkin and chop the flesh into ½-inch cubes. Place the pumpkin in a saucepan with the orange zest and juice and the lemon juice. Bring to a boil, cover with a tight-fitting lid, and simmer gently for 10–15 minutes or until the pumpkin is tender. Allow to cool slightly then place the pumpkin and juice in a food processor or blender and blend until smooth. Return to the pan.

3 Blend the cornstarch with the water and add to the pan with ⅓ cup of the sugar. Cook, stirring, for about 3 minutes until the mixture is thick and bubbling. Pour into the pastry shell and level the surface.

4 Whisk the egg whites in a bowl until stiff. Gradually whisk in the remaining sugar, a little at a time and whisking well between each addition. Spoon the meringue over the filling and swirl with an offset spatula. Return to the oven for a further 5–8 minutes until lightly browned. Allow to cool before serving.

serves 8

sweet pumpkin fritters
with spiced vanilla cream

preparation time: 15 minutes
cooking time: about 10 minutes

- ⅔ cup heavy cream
- 1 teaspoon vanilla extract
- ½ teaspoon ground cinnamon
- 4 teaspoons superfine sugar
- 1½ lbs pumpkin, seeded
- 2 tablespoons lemon juice

BATTER:

- ¾ cup all-purpose flour

- 2 tablespoons superfine sugar
- 2 eggs, separated
- ½ cup cold water
- vegetable or peanut oil, for frying
- extra sugar, for dusting

1 Lightly whip the cream in a bowl with the vanilla, cinnamon, and 2 teaspoons of the sugar until soft peaks form. Transfer to a small serving dish and chill.

2 Cut off the skin from the pumpkin and slice the flesh into chunky pieces, about ¾-inch wide. Toss in a bowl with the remaining sugar and the lemon juice.

3 For the batter, put the flour and sugar in a mixing bowl. Add the egg yolks and the cold water. Whisk to a smooth batter. Whisk the egg whites until peaks form, then fold into the batter with a large metal spoon.

4 Heat 1½ inches of oil in a heavy-based frying pan until a teaspoon of the batter sizzles and rises to the surface. Drop several of the pumpkin pieces into the batter and then lift out with a fork so the excess batter falls back into the bowl. Lower the battered pumpkin pieces carefully into the oil. Sauté for 2–3 minutes until golden. Drain on paper towels while cooking the rest.

5 Sprinkle with extra sugar and serve with the spiced vanilla cream.

serves 4–6

cinnamon and pumpkin pancakes
with gingered crème fraîche

preparation time: 15 minutes
cooking time: 10–15 minutes

- 2 pieces crystallized ginger, finely chopped
- 1 cup crème fraîche
- 1 lb pumpkin, seeded
- 2 eggs
- 1 cup all-purpose flour
- 1 teaspoon ground cinnamon
- ½ cup light brown sugar
- vegetable or peanut oil, for shallow frying

1 Mix together the crystallized ginger and crème fraîche and put into a small serving dish.

2 Cut the pumpkin into small pieces, discarding the skin. Steam over a pan of gently simmering water for about 20 minutes until just tender. Allow to cool slightly then place in a food processor or blender and blend to a smooth puree.

3 Add the eggs, flour, cinnamon, and sugar and blend until smooth.

4 Heat a little oil in a large, heavy-based frying pan. Place several spoonfuls of the mixture in the pan, spacing them slightly apart, and sauté gently until golden on the bottom. Turn the pancakes over and cook until just firm. Transfer to a warm plate while cooking the remaining batter. Serve warm with the gingered crème fraîche.

serves 4

variation

Spoon maple syrup over the pumpkin pancakes as an alternative to the gingered crème fraîche.

sticky pumpkin and bananas
with vanilla ice cream

preparation time: 5 minutes
cooking time: 7 minutes

- 14 oz pumpkin, seeded
- 3 tablespoons unsalted butter
- 2 tablespoons superfine
  sugar
- finely grated zest and juice of
  1 small orange

- 2 large bananas, each cut
  diagonally into quarters
- ¼ cup golden raisins
- 8 scoops of vanilla ice cream,
  slightly softened

1 Remove the skin from the pumpkin and cut the flesh into ¼-inch thick slices. Melt the butter in a frying pan and sauté the pumpkin slices for 2–3 minutes on each side until lightly browned and softened.

2 Add the sugar and heat gently, stirring, until the sugar dissolves. Cook for 1–2 minutes until the sugar starts to color.

3 Add the orange zest and juice, bananas, and golden raisins and cook gently for 2 minutes, stirring. Spoon over the ice cream in shallow bowls.

serves 4

caramelized pumpkin
with coconut rice pudding

preparation time: 10 minutes
cooking time: 35 minutes

- ¾ cup pudding rice
- 14 oz can coconut milk
- 1 cup milk
- 2 bay leaves
- ¼ cup superfine sugar

PUMPKIN:

- 13 oz pumpkin, seeded
- 3 tablespoons unsalted butter
- 3 tablespoons superfine
  sugar

1 Put the rice in a heavy-based saucepan with the coconut milk, milk, bay leaves, and sugar. Bring slowly to a boil, stirring. Reduce to the lowest possible heat, partially cover with a lid, and simmer very gently for 30 minutes, stirring frequently, until the rice is tender and the mixture is thickened and pulpy. Add a little more milk if the pudding starts to dry out.

2 While the rice is cooking, remove the rind from the pumpkin. Cut the flesh into ¼-inch thick slices. Blanch the slices in boiling water for 2 minutes until softened but not falling apart. Drain.

3 Melt the butter in a frying pan. Add the sugar and cook, stirring, until the sugar dissolves, then cook without stirring until the mixture starts to brown. Add the pumpkin slices and cook gently, turning the pumpkin in the buttery syrup until tender, about 3 minutes.

4 Remove the bay leaves once the rice is cooked. Spoon the rice into bowls and top with the pumpkin slices and syrup.

serves 4

cook's tip _____

The bay leaves aren't essential in the rice pudding but they do give it a lovely aromatic flavor. Leave them out if you prefer. Keep an eye on the rice when you start cooking it because the milk can boil over if set on too high a heat.

pumpkin and apricot conserve

preparation time: 15 minutes, plus soaking
cooking time: 25 minutes

- 6 oz dried apricots, quartered
- ½ cup fresh orange juice
- 1½ lbs pumpkin, seeded
- 1¼ cups superfine sugar

1 Put the apricots and orange juice in a bowl, cover with plastic wrap and leave in a cool place overnight until the apricots absorb most of the juice.

2 Cut the pumpkin into small cubes, discarding the skin. Put in a heavy-based saucepan with the apricots, juice, and sugar and heat gently, stirring, until the sugar dissolves. Cook gently, uncovered, for about 25 minutes until the pumpkin is tender and the syrup thickened. Transfer to a clean jar or bowl and allow to cool completely.

3 This conserve can be stored in the refrigerator for up to 2 weeks.

makes 1½ lbs

cook's tip

Serve this sweet conserve-like jam with bread or toast, or as a topping for yogurt. Alternatively, warm through and serve with ice cream.

pumpkin and raisin chutney

preparation time: 15 minutes
cooking time: about 45 minutes

- 2 lbs pumpkin, seeded
- 1 large onion, chopped
- 1 large cooking apple, cored and grated
- 1¼ cup raisins
- 1¾ cups white wine vinegar

- 1½ cups light brown sugar
- 1½ oz fresh ginger, grated
- 2 teaspoons salt
- 2 cinnamon sticks, halved
- 2 tablespoons coriander seeds, lightly crushed

1 Cut the pumpkin into ¾-inch chunks, discarding the skin.

2 Put the pumpkin in a large, heavy-based saucepan and add all the remaining ingredients. Bring to a boil, stirring frequently. Reduce the heat and cook gently, uncovered, for about 45 minutes until the chutney is thick and pulpy. To check whether the chutney is cooked, draw a wooden spoon through the mixture, it should leave a clean trail on the base of the pan that slowly disappears.

3 Spoon the chutney into sterilized jars and cover with waxed discs and lids. Store in a cool place for a month before using.

makes 2½ lbs

cook's tips

To sterilize glass jars, thoroughly clean the jars, removing any old labels, and heat in a low oven, 300°F, for 15 minutes. Alternatively, use jars straight from a hot dishwasher cycle.

This quantity makes a small amount of chutney but can easily be doubled. You should increase the cooking time slightly.

turkish pumpkin candy

preparation time: 10 minutes
cooking time: 25 minutes

- 2 lb wedge from a large
  pumpkin, seeded
- ⅔ cup light brown sugar
- ¼ cup water

- ¼ cup rosewater
- 2 tablespoons lemon juice
- ½ cup pistachio nuts, roughly
  chopped, with skins removed

1 Cut the pumpkin into large chunks, discarding the skin. Place in a heavy-based saucepan and add the sugar and water. Heat gently, stirring, until the sugar dissolves. Cook, uncovered, over a gentle heat for about 25 minutes, stirring frequently, until the pumpkin is very tender and the syrup is very thick.

2 Stir in the rosewater and lemon juice and serve sprinkled with the pistachio nuts.

serves 6

cook's tip

This makes a delicious sweet treat served with a swirl of thick yogurt or lightly whipped cream.

toasted pumpkin seeds

preparation time: 5 minutes
cooking time: 3 minutes

- ¼ stick (2 tablespoons)
  unsalted butter
- 1 cup pumpkin seeds

- ¼ cup sunflower seeds
- 1 teaspoon ground cinnamon
- ¼ cup superfine sugar

1 Melt the butter in a frying pan. Add the pumpkin seeds and sunflower seeds, cinnamon, and sugar.

2 Cook over a gentle heat, stirring constantly, for 2–3 minutes until the sugary butter has turned into a caramel and the seeds are beginning to pop.

3 Transfer to a bowl and allow to cool. Mix with a fork to break up any seeds that may have stuck together.

makes 1¼ cups

cook's tip

These mixed seeds make a great alternative to chips and nuts for nibbling. They're also good sprinkled over ice cream or scattered onto breakfast cereals.